This Is My Body

This Is My Body

poems by

Terry Song

For Alexandra —
Many of these poems
you know from workshop —
Love,
Terry
2/16/94

West End Press

Grateful acknowledgment is given to the following publications in which some of the poems were previously published:

The Maryland Poetry Review: "A Prayer for Peace"

Puerto del Sol: "Into the Light," "Why Men Talk Politics and Can't Seem to Get Close to Each Other" and "Road Kill No. 2"

Blue Mesa Review: "Two Women in a Pear Tree Swinging" and "In Bread We Trust"

Whole Notes: "The Woman Who Stayed" (previously titled "unspoken dialogue")

Cielo Azul: "Grace," "Beside the Midnight Llano" and "Thieving Flowers"

Rio Grande Review: "How to Raise Kids" and "Our Hands"

Special thanks:

—to Joe Somoza, Kathleene West and Keith Wilson for their help and support;

—to Debbi, Donna, Karen, Lori, Leona and Bobby for their attentive and sensitive reading of this manuscript in its early stages;

—and to my babysitters, without whose help none of this would have been possible.

First edition, January 1994
ISBN 0-931122-77-5

Cover art by Andrea Adams
Book design by Michael Reed
Typography by Prototype

West End Press • P.O. Box 27334 • Albuquerque, NM 87125

Contents

—for my mother and grandmothers,

for all the women, living and dead, who influenced me,

and especially for Emily, who first gave me the dream
of living hidden away in the New England woods
and being an American poet

Unfolding

If I could see the crafting
of my life like
the love of shaping
letters, rounding the o's
then letting go, allowing them to
open to smooth
curves of c's and u's,
draw in again, then rise above,
ascending d's and transcendent
b's becoming, forgiving
the cross t, the crucified
x, to let it unwind in
slow sinuous lines, to
snake the smooth back of s.

Life Expectancy

Why Men Talk Politics
and Can't Seem to Get Close to Each Other

The trouble with men is
not that they don't eat
quiche or have babies;
they never danced together
in bedrooms like their
sisters, never
rolled the rug back, locked
arms in a polka, laughing,
careening round the
room, draped
arms about a shoulder or waist or
embraced in the soft
slowness of jazz.
In their trenches and
forts with pretend
sandbags they put
distance between themselves at
10, elbows in ribs, tackle at 13,
whipping each other's butts
behind the school. They were
cruising at 16. Cruising for
what? Not
Saturday night slumber
parties, not
jitterbug with the boys
where they could have dropped
the needle on a favorite
45, clicked on the
radio to late night KOMA Oklahoma
City, never once caring who
saw or who danced with
whom or how close or how they
looked—only
the music
surging through bare
feet on a wood
floor, hands

joined, soft hair
flying, young
bodies
dreaming
a new dance.

Only a Daughter?

"No," she said,
if she'd had a girl,
it probably would have looked like Huck
Finn, and someone would've called
Social Services. Boys were
easy, what does it matter, we're all
human beings. When she was
pregnant and people inquired,
"As long as it's healthy," she replied but almost
cried when the Girl Scouts rode by on their
float in the Harvest Parade holding
hands and singing, their voices thin
and light as the breath of angels.
When her friend's grown daughter became
pregnant with her first child,
she knew it wasn't the frills
and curls she would miss, but
plain as a boulder in the desert
and deep this need to pass on
accumulated experience, the voices
whose names are dust, who
sing to the unborn
daughters—and her own
coming to womanhood, the liberation
of college days, not waiting
for the guy to tune her
car or ask her to dance, and how
she learned to ask,
learned to speak her
mind, discovered how to move her body
to the music in her own head,
and after many seasons of her
hands in the soil, how to
love and let grow,
push a baby from her
body and nurse it
and love.

Two women in a pear tree swinging

and behind them the spread blanket
of Oklahoma hills, the rolling
farmland billowed out like a patched
quilt bleached white by the hard
sun. And the pear tree,
old as a gnarled grandma,
spanning the pale rebozo sky, rooted
deep in the dark soil,
bears her thousand children
and the two women aloft
in a circle of shade.

From a sagging green daybed
on the screened-in porch I watch
in the perfect stillness of noon.
The salty taste of sweat
erases all trace of lunch's
cold peach jam
on fat slabs of homemade bread.
I twitch a fly, crank up my
elbows on the pillow, press
back the hot breath that
prickles on my skin, Indian
summer hung heavily with the
sweet and sour incense of ripe
berries, of peppers and tomatoes and
the honeysuckle vine twining
fingers blooming russet
darting emerald
hummingbird
gladiola
tangerine.

Everything ripens
to the hum of the fan in the front room,
the buzz of hollyhocks.
And the large limb groans with the
weight of the women swinging.

Their low voices run
up the scale and drift
down like feathers in the
heavy afternoon. The younger one trails
a slender foot in the silky grass.
A checkered tail of gingham dress
flutters with the breeze of the swinging
rhythm of the tree murmuring ceaseless
flow of the women talking
they nod their heads
as though falling
asleep, as though
falling through some dream.

Still She Marches through Bataan

I fold clothes at the Salvation Army,
arrange men's shorts, the children's
pants and summer tops. I smooth
curtains stacked in bins behind the
yellow storefront glass. She walks
past. "Crazy Mary," people
whisper, and I wonder,
what is her real name?

The old-timers in this town say
she once stood tall in her crisp
white, her shining hair
french-rolled beneath the
cap, the half-moon marks
of oval nails, her firm
fingers on their pulse.
They remember a cool hand
binding their wounds, soothing the
cheek of a fevered child.
Such a long time, they sigh,
long time since the war, when she
signed up with their boys and came
back to them this stranger, the starched
white crumpled to brown layered on
brown on her stooped frame, her ashen
face and the wild
brush of her steelwool hair
scratching the eyes of day
and her own black pits.

Now, her dirty nails
bit to the quick, her hand
clenches a stubby pencil while she
walks these streets with her
clipboard and its big black marks,
the angry rows of heavy lines as she cries,
"James Humphrey Hill, three thousand six,
Jesus Valdez, three thousand seven,"

and she flings her curses in the
street, her own strong hands
turned to sieves.

From the cash register, from the men's
pants people laugh.
"Crazy Mary," they say
and turn their faces away
from what you bear,
the numbers of death,
the names
that fell too
quick on black soil.

Into the Light

Among the garden paths
and patches of lawn
the women move
laying out sleeping bags
tucked up under grapevines
or by some low wall
in preparation for the night.

The sun dips low
beyond the tangle of cottonwood
and we retreat to the old barn
to ourselves
this circle
of quiet
waiting.

We think of Nena
now in prison
because as a nurse in Tucson
caring for her children
putting her husband through
graduate school she
helped some refugees from
El Salvador.

"I send my strength to Nena,"
says one brown-haired
mother teacher student
who begins her day long before
light in a steamy shower,
sits sipping predawn coffee,
curtains open. "I gather my
strength in darkness," she says,
"while the world still sleeps."

"The power you harvest in
darkness I get from the sun,"
says one who works indoors.
"With the sun on my face

I recharge my own solar
cells." She reminds us
of that evening we
christened the adobe house
Manny and Gail built by the
river. With boughs and
branches of juniper we
danced around the house
brushing and shaking
shaking and brushing out
unwanted spirits from corners
and dark closets.

And yes what I remember
is the sun   later
as we stood outside
the sun touching the open field
of wheat, fire reflecting
red earth in our gleaming skin.

And the late sun's orange glow
deepens in the dusty silence
while someone remembers Vivian
claimed by cancer
how last year she led us
in the dance of Sarah's circle
as we danced the four directions
celebrated Juniper's passage
into womanhood, crowned her
with a wildflower wreath
and the gentle rain.

Viv danced the earth
and the sap of the green willow
rising, defying gravity.
She would have said:
"I will lift up mine eyes
unto the hills from whence
cometh my strength."

On and on around the circle
from bare palms women offer
sturdy coins of sun and moon

finer alloys: men and children,
sorrow and dreaming,
till the ring grows smaller, the women
draw in, shoulders pressing tight
the last light through the slats
of the barn
and an energy
centuries old

lifts up a holy song

and the women move.

Alleluia for the Kitchen Singers

—for fortnightly bathing
and glee

a womb inside rock
walls on a dusty
street in San Lorenzo, an open

window and thin threads of voices
tuning among the red
trumpets, the honeysuckled throats

in the overhanging
vines a ruffle of breeze,
chatter of coffeepot,

a hummingbird hums, the late afternoon
sun in glasses of wine
on the wornsmooth table,

a cast iron kettle on the woodstove
        one voice begins

wooden spoons and spatulas in a crock
        another joins in

a fruited basket hanging
        and another voice, another

                dimension, dark and bright
                threads weaving
                a song for ancestors

the generations pasted in
pictures on the wall, beneath
magnets on the fridge

                a winged song for
                children that startles like
                blackbirds from a pie

a large poster where a woman
kneels on green earth, flowers
bloom down the boughs of her arms,

she offers them to the kitchen
singers, leaned back in chairs,
they sing for her dark

eyes that follow them as they
nod and dip and sway, eight
women, their one body chiming

    alleluias like bells
    down the dark branch of night

Marion's Poem

Morning behind her house,
the cholla-stemmed
hillside slopes to oak.
Metal lawn chairs under
juniper, the steam
from her coffee
rises to early
blue from cupped hands.
Earlier than her rooster
or one that answers
from down the valley, she
sits with binoculars,
Peterson's Field Guide
on the cable spool beside her.
Before farmers,
before the first truck whines
down the road, she
begins in silence, in clear
air watching for migrants headed
south: a flock of geese, a blue
heron up river, mostly
juncos,
towhees,
a Townsend's warbler,
her neighbors she calls them.
Sometimes she greets a stranger,
flips the color plates, eager
to call her guest by name,
begins her day a child
delighting in blue
and yellow feathers.

Speaking of Seasons

Snuggled under the covers with my infant
son, I startled
when she burst into the room. In a voice
bright as the white cuffs
peeking from her red sweater sleeves,
she announced, Today
is Juniper's 17th birthday!
and perched on the bed, knees to
chest, mid-September in her
face and soft hair; come from
morning with her daughter, a breakfast
of tortillas and eggs, hot
coffee and biscochos
and the gift she had
wrapped in blue tissue.

Seventeen years ago today—
she unfolded her story—Juniper was
born in the old boxcar where we
made our first home
and planted a garden.

It was the first killing
frost when she had labored unaware
that the cold earth contracted,
gripping the live roots of
cornstalks in her garden,
and next morning
had wandered out among frozen
melons and tomato vines.
The world
changed in a night.
Beanstalks to diamonds,
a transformation of
pumpkins, light
fairy dust of snow. And inside,
by the woodstove, in a laundry basket
nestled in blankets and soft rags,
their Juniper.

Seventeen.   She shook her head in
wonder at the sound of it.
I snuggled deeper below warm
covers with my baby and held him
close.   I squeezed his fat leg.
Again,
like a child whispering the name of
God: seventeen,
as if it were something
holy, as if
how could she not have
known in those long, slow
days in her garden by the elm how
quickly seedlings grow, the harvest
comes and nests empty.

life expectancy

When the moment came,
the clerk's hands
poised over the register,
I could not let her ring up
the thirty-two dollars for
the skirt, a perfect
fit in acid-washed
denim, the rage that year;

but when it came right
down to the bottom
line on the skirt tag, I
had to put it
back on the rack for someone
else to buy, someone who might not even
see that it said

"Made in Bangladesh"
by a woman who made pennies
maybe thirty-two each day she
spent washing skirts
in a steamy hot
factory, the thin
cloth of her burkha
sticking to her damp hair, without
air conditioning or toilets,
and the acid
fumes, the weight of wet
denim, her thin arms
lifting it.

She counted herself lucky;
a third of her friends had
died before age five,
another third had not survived
childbirth—and she,
praise Allah!
of the remaining

was the one to get a job
washing denim:
she could feed her children
till her ripe old age,
dying at forty-nine if she
continued to be lucky.

I apologized to the clerk and
left, thinking at forty-nine I could
start a new job or move to a different
city, fly to visit kids
in college or Canada, bicycle
east or hike south.
My heels clicked out
questions on the tiles
as I left the mall,
and my old skirt hung
loose on my hips
when I walked out.

Grace

Not because she was worthy, or even
paying attention, she was only pumping
gas in her car before the usual
rush to the sitter's, both
kids in the back seat.
Like a penny hidden by a child
in the crack of a sidewalk
for an unsuspecting stranger to find,
regardless of merit, it was
just as she lifted the nozzle
toward its cradle in the pump,
out of the corner of her
eye she received the gift,
headed south on foot
down the street,
black-crested, red-
masked:

a white-ringed pheasant!

For a moment, the nozzle
suspended in mid-air, her breath hung
white in the cold, and the children's heads
lifted, their round faces lit like wild
sunflowers, and the station windows
freeze-framed the man counting
change to a woman, both faces
turned as though
someone had called their
names. At 8:32 a.m. on Espina Street
the morning converged in clear
light that spun
gold in the hair of the woman at the
pump, shone
glittering through station
windows, car windows, like a magic
stained glass church turning
everyday faces into shining holy

saints, blazing
the body of pheasant,
iridescent, brown-
speckled, to fire.

When visiting Chicago

if you're looking for golden loaves
of turtles or alligators,
horseshoes or wedding breads
braided with roses and leaves,
the place to go is St. Germain's.
If you're dreaming of a starfish
or a mosque of burnished
walls, looped and beaded, brown-
kneaded, take a walk down to State Street
near Division to the yellow awnings, sidewalk
tables, bundles of wheat in the window,
and the bowls made of bread, the small
loaves of bacon and
herbs, cheese and rye,
pain á sportif with hazelnuts,
pain ècolier, au familial, pain complet,
croissants au chocolat.

But if you catch the wrong
El headed south past
Chinatown and you notice
this isn't Old Town,
no veneer on these burned-out
buildings, broken
windows, where a child gets on,
the sores around his
mouth bursting with pus,
he sings his little
rap for your entertainment
about a boy whose baby
sister was eaten by
rats, and you don't know whether
to look him in the eyes as he sings
or look at your own feet,
and the black woman across the aisle
watches to see what the white
mother will do. He holds out his

cup. You look in his face,
where one eye wanders, and you
wonder whether to
drop in all your quarters or
give him the golden loaves.

You give him the change, knowing it won't change
anything.
You find the right train
back. This time you try
the vanilla salambo or passion fruit
Bavarian, Mirabelle tart or mocha
eclair; you try a cup of espresso
or cappucino, thinking you can
cut the bitterness
with cream at St. Germain's.

Despair is a Luxury

When it's not quite light yet,
and despair is a luxury you can't
live with, begin with
singing. Throw open your
curtains. Let in the darkness.
When you've just put on the coffee,
you open the paper, first thing
is: "Subterranean Nukes Penetrate
Earth's Crust Before Bursting."
On page 6 is life
expectancy for Third World
women, late 40s and the Murrays
in Stantonville, Texas,
population 4,000 who have no
clues to their 8 year old Maggie's
whereabouts,
last seen on her way to the local
grocery, a block from home.

When night's fingers threaten
to choke the white breath of morning
and the restless
treading in your gut won't
stop, even though
your
children are safe in
bed, their lunchpails
full, clothes
clean, waiting for school,
begin with singing.
It doesn't
matter if you sing
the blues or a lullaby or even
the Mine Workers' Union Song;
it can be at the kitchen
table or on your back
porch. The trick is to

sing for your own full
breasts and the solid
boat of your bed with its billowed
sheets;
hang
each note
whole
to shine in the dark.

In These Times

How to Raise Kids

i.

It's okay if they scream their lungs out
when they're a baby and you've
nursed and rocked and walked already.

When they cry to a slather of sweat
soaking the nightshirt, plastering
a slick hair cap to their head,

then you can go in, lay them back
down, rub their belly; they should
sleep like a baby.

Maybe all night.

ii.

Let them flip their own pancake,
check for brownness on one side, then
the other, make their own

sandwich if they're 8 years
old and whining about
socks that don't feel right

and tennies with the heels broken
down because they're too
lazy to untie them first.

"And what will you give me if I do?"

iii.

Teach them if you
can the end of a
hoehandle, the smell of

fish and old
broccoli in undumped
trash, the oily

feel of a dustrag in their
own hands on their
furniture. And by all means—

a week at Grandma's.

iv.

They must write their own
story, even if it's the
grandma who meets a prince

and one adventure is strung to
the next with nary a
comma much less a full

stop or a breath and all the
words are so phonetic that only
the kid can read it.

They must revise their own story.

v.

Let me know, will you
(all of you who were still
childless when you swore

never to let them eat
sugar or watch T.V., to do things
different from your parents, teach them

"Yes!" instead of "No! Don't!"), did you

plug into cable after all and buy them G.I.
Joe? Did you yell "No!"
when small hands reached

for a hot stove, when feet
headed for the street or profanity
sprouted from young mouths?

vi.

I need your advice
on the resolution of
crisis, splinters in tender

feet, trips to the dentist.
And if the body is beautiful and sex is
good (as we all know) and

natural (as you always said), do you
still run naked through the
house? do you

lock the bedroom door?

The Allowance Jar

It wasn't exactly stealing.
She was his mom after all
and usually when she
asked if she could
borrow a dollar or so,
"Just take all you want.
I really don't need it,"
he would say, then
offer up the jar.

But this time
she went into his
room while he was
at school and without
asking scooped out
the last dollar
(not without hesitation
and the thought of how many
times she had said, "If you
don't clean your room, you won't
get your allowance,"
of course her eyes sweeping
the spiffed up room, and
damn! why hadn't she
paid him back those other
times so there'd be
more to "borrow" now?)
and she shook the last
coins into her pocket.

When her son came
home, when he
raced to his room
to grab two quarters
for the ice cream
man, he ran
tearing to her room yelling
right in her face demanding

to know, "WHO STOLD MY
MONEY?" screaming,
"WHERE'S ALL MY DOLLARS?"
his eyes burning,
small hands holding
up the empty jar, her heart
sinking as she mumbled
something about
"borrowing"
and some other words.

You

Before we bought the new house
you were the one who stayed
awake to toss the coins. Bent
over the Book of Changes,
between cupped hands
you shook them, eyes
fixed beyond the wall, asking
"Is this the right move for us?"
And in patterns of broken
and solid lines you watched for
signs. Yes, you

who bent to sniff the
first pale iris by the door,
the thin cloud of hair floating
up from your head, how the sun
shone through it, through your
gold-brickle eyes. After we

bought the new house you caught your
son as he slipped between my
legs into life. "Oh, little frog,"
you whispered, your eyes wet as you
placed him on my belly, held his brother up
to touch him. It was always

you, in the new house or
old, washing
dishes late at night, dreaming
in our small kitchen your plans
to save the world. Then later
you coming in to rub my
shoulders, my back, rub me
down with almond oil. Oh,
anoint me with warm hands!

In These Times

*You who were
are no longer and what I was I'm not.
Am I to know myself?*

—Marvin Bell
"You Would Know"

"Step on a crack, you will
break your mother's
back," children
chanted on the schoolyard
sidewalk. Was it too many
children in cracks that finally
wore your heart to the thinness of trying
to keep them in shoes
and oranges, much less
in tow Sunday mornings, having put
rolls on to rise, cut up a
hen to fry for the preacher over
after, while you
hurried the five girls, Grandpa
leaning on the Model T horn, shouting,
"Jewel, don't you have those kids ready
yet!" You handed the four boys
hankies, dimes for the collection plate,
and pinning hat to head and
humming, strode out to
meet impatient eyes.

This rare weekend of escape to the lake,
alone on the small dock and my children
clambering like crabs up the sandy
slope back to the cabin—
you were twenty years
older than I am now
that last day you watched us
scrabble up the same steep
slope, dangling
your legs from the dock's
edge, your hair

already escaping the white straw
hat. You laughed,
"I think I could live
forever."

And oh! the next morning
when Aunt Betty shook Grandpa away, crying
"Papa! Papa! Mama's dead!"
I was a sorry river
shrivelled to salt,
a heart heaving and cracking
like boulders in the arroyo
when rain comes too fast.
Such loss was everything
when I was eleven. Why
did it have to be you? And still,
so many questions:

Who would you be now
in this age as mass
collapses to infinite density, time
accelerates, tracking the speed of
light across our backs?
I need to know.
Our families are small.
No one home to sow
seeds or gather eggs.
Who could even tell
a story? What steady
hands to guide small fingers
in the knotting of thread,
the stitching of hems?

I need you now as you were
then when the waters
flowed below your pasture and squirrels
chattered through your
tree. I need your creeks
that swell in the
spring, creeks with
trees that dangle grapevines and roped
sandbags to swing on.

If I could see you
in the thin morning light,
coming from henhouse, apron
full of brown eggs, a fat
hen by the feet, wings
splayed from your hands,
then I might know.

But your apricot jam is gone.
Even the old ladies don't roll down their
stockings anymore. And the boxes of
dresses and hats you gave us,
the handbags and high-heeled
shoes have gone
the way of all playthings.

How am I to know
what street to raise my
kids on? The stars can point a way,
but city lights confuse.
Prices are high, and the calendar
falls in on itself.
Please, come
sit awhile with me; we can blame
the thoughtless Oklahoma summer
days that unfolded so slowly
I could not get here in time
to ask you these things.

Salvation

What is heaven anyway,
but when we play our little
game and I cry,

''Boo Hoo!
I need you!''

or sometimes it's
"Help! Help!"

and you fling your arms round
my neck, press your cheek
hard and shout,

''I saved you, Mom!''
then I have to say, "Thank you,

Corey," and wrap you up, "Oh!
thank you!''

From the Edge

The drone of grownups
snoring in two double beds in the same
room, a week of fishing
for bass at Lake Kemp when I was
10, my cousins
on cots in rows, their pale cotton
pajamas, small faces
white in the full moon light, moon
licking at cracks in the one-room
cabin, the little moaning
cries of night, the wind
whipping up white
foam on the lake, lapping
at the edges of my dream.

> There's a boat moving
> fast, lightly
> skimming the water, the man
> at the wheel is smiling and waving
> like in a photograph.
> The wind of speeding makes his
> hair fly out—and the day,
> wide open and bright before him.
> Behind him
> a skier falls and he circles
> back, suddenly
> stands on the edge of the boat with heavy
> boots and no
> lifebelt
>   and not because the fallen
>   skier needs rescue, bobbing
>   safely in his orange
>   life preserver,
>   but like it is
>   written in his script, his large
> body leaps from the edge, his shirt
> lifts and hairy belly hangs

suspended before the huge
splash and water, slow
motion,
flinging out in drops when he bobs and
vanishes like the dark
rings of water.

I am only 10,
and I forget about the dream as soon as my cousins
wake me, hurry to eat your cornflakes,
and the fight over who gets to ride in
the boat to check the trotlines,
until my large uncle drowns
that day.   Something orange
bobbing
bobbing,
heavy boots and a wild
leap into darkness.
The keening
wail of my aunt lingers
after dusk on the lake.
For a long
time I am afraid
to dream.

Road Kill No. 2

You remember your first
road kill when you were fifteen,
summer of 9th grade, driving
home the eleven miles, wide
open country highway in your parents'
Delta 98 and Mrs. Whitecotton's
whole flock of chickens coming
up out of a dip in the road.
Instant head-on, no chance to
brake or swerve, just
keeping it on the road, and the sickening
thunk ka thunk ka thunk of chickens'
heads and the feel of their soft bodies
thudding under the car. Your hands
froze to the wheel, you could
barely keep your lunch down, couldn't take your
eyes off the rearview
mirror, you knew you should
stop. Mrs. Whitecotton was your nearest
neighbor, and she knew your parents. She was your
history teacher, and these were her fine White
Leghorns and Auracanas,
but the car kept barreling
forward like a tank and the bar ditch
at the road's edge was really
steep with no place to turn
around. Geez—you had barely got your
driver's license, and what was
a high school girl to do,
stop in the middle of the highway
and chase the ruined hens
down with their flopping
heads, blood spurting, feathers
flying all over the place? What if
traffic had come
or Mrs. Whitecotton?

In Memory of the White Mountain Ice Cream Bucket

Three rusty rings
fall from dried oak slats
like the days,
scattering the thunderburst
evenings of summers, colored
bolts of our songs like
silk unrolling down the valley.
A madrigal. A song for children.
From the rock house
porch on Bluejay Hill, a straight shot
south to Cooke's Peak, a few
junipers, some friends tipping
glasses of homemade wine from valley
mint and Black Twig apples. While someone
sits on the salted ice
the others take turns at cranking fresh
cream and vanilla, sing
"White Coral Bells" slowly;
and the freezing begins.
With a down, down,
hey, derry down it's
triple-time, till the bucket's
inched to the porch edge; arms
aching, reel it down andante
for "Old King Cole," then
largo "Alleluia" it's ice cream,
almonds, ripe peaches
frothing out of the lid, and the
moon rises full, the singers
soak the open
pores of the night sky.

The Last Chapter

i.

He was a big old man
but wiry and hard
coming in from the peanut fields
overalls drooping
hoarfrost hair bristling
from his nose.

Thirty chickens, three dogs.
Nine kids close together
in the church pew every Sunday,
yes, sir.
Hard Times.
And he couldn't buy them shoes or
oranges for Christmas.

ii.

Then we came along and he
tickled us till we cried
chased us to the cane patch
grossed us all out
with his song of Fanny Bright (or
was it Fanny Britches?),
> "O-o-oh-h-h . . .
> I went to see my girl
> a pleasure I was seekin'
> missed 'er mouth and
> kissed 'er nose
> the darn thing started leakin'."

iii.

Things changed when Grandma died,
but he carried on alone
put his jam in the county fair
making all those old crones mad
with his blue ribbons.
Even made his own tamales
from the local squirrels
till he finally forgot
where he kept the lard.

And how could we keep from laughing
the time he came to visit
for a week, and
in his suitcase
only cornhusks
and old yellow chickenfeet.

"Oh well," we said
because even then
he still could win at checkers
or Scrabble, read the Bible and
the Almanac with his
dime-store glasses.

And still he kept on planting
in rhythm with the moon
till they finally moved him
        to a little house
        on the edge of town
        and sold his farm.

iv.

And you won't find him if you
go there now it's
bigger,
better,
lots of shoes and
oil where there used to be the shade of
vineyards, orchards patched to cornrows
wild green blankets
spreading out for
the feet of children running
to the creek.

We are all kids in Oklahoma

waiting for Uncle Kenneth to say
"Let's hunt wangdoodles in the
cane patch. You kids go ahead.
I'll be right behind you."
Hiding our smiles, suspending
disbelief, we race to the patch
behind the henhouse, to paths that
part themselves open and with dry
whispers swallow us whole.
Into a dust dark world, we
lose each other in the
maze of narrow tracks.

We are all kids in Oklahoma
thirsting, and our hearts beat fast.
We long to be the first
to glimpse the strange
beast. We hold our breath
and listen
for the tense laughter of our
cousins, the soft crackling of
footfalls in the dry cane.
The stalks shake wildly,
always just ahead, an almost human
cry from a shadowed form. Our screams
catch in our open throats as we
run for the edge
away from the dark heart.

In Bread We Trust

A Prayer for Peace

What we need now is bread,
soft dough to dig
fingers in, to knuckle and
pinch, pummel and punch
down. Like the grass
when crushed under foot
springing back,
it will not cry out or
die like daughters
and sons.
If we must raise our
fists, let us
plunge them in the body
of yeast and wheat.
Bread is not flesh.
Our hands will come
clean if we rise like
acre upon acre of shining
grain. Let us be sun-
ripe and light
like the crusty
loaves. Let us break
bread.

Nectarine

Peeling nectarines to make a pie,
the gift of a neighbor's
bounty, some sliced on
screens to dry in sunny
windows of our van for winter
treats or chopped up in sweet
breads, several perfect ones
laid aside to eat fresh,
and these,
in the sink, the bruised
and broken, somewhere my finger
plunges through soft ooze of over-
ripe, others with good
parts to be peeled and cut
or bit off and eaten till it's
nothing wasted and it's on my
chin, dripping off my
elbows—oh,
sweet nectarine! it's still
summer and the cooler
hums while I prepare to make pie.
Though I might have to turn it off.
The wind is scratching music,
mesquite limbs on the window, dark
clouds blowing
something in from the east.

Beside the Midnight Llano

i.

Do you remember those first hours
on the porch of the old frame house?
Me on the step with my legs
tucked up and you stretched
out on the ground nearby
under stars under the
influence we talked
families meanings
ourselves unraveled
into the dark llano across the
pasture the harvest
moon as we walked
climbed up the groaning
windmill up dream
ladders the soft
hoot of burrowing owl
and we wondered
who who

ii.

It was too late
for you to drive
back to town you
said "I'll just
camp out in the yard."
And you did
while I sat up
played the guitar
tried to read
the restless night
wondering were you asleep
humming singing a little
with the light on to let you
know I was awake.
And you

wide awake in your
bedroll tiptoed to my
window tapping timidly
asking me could I bring you some
carrot sticks.

iii.

Me beside you on the
grass awkwardly
munched carrots
as though an
everynight ritual
man and woman
crunching carrots
beside the midnight llano.
We tried quickly to
finish, then
broke into laughter.
"It really wasn't
carrot sticks I wanted,"
you whispered lightly,
opened a slice of
moon on my breast.

Cliff Dweller

Only the sound
of the river below,
and the canyon wren
flits from oak branch
to her nest in the high
cliff. In the wall
on a lip of hardpressed
earth, a woman
sits sunwarmed before
the wind-scooped
face of her home,
her glistening black
hair drawn into braids,
her wrists that rise and
fall, that rock in slow
motion grinding
corn in her metate,
the mano shaped to hand,
to the rhythm of
breath.
She lifts an earthen
olla to her shoulder;
the voice of leaves,
rumors whispered among
trees, echo within.
Her eyes gather
the swift feet of clouds
climbing up the sky.
Her feet
know their own way
down the worn
holes in the rough
wall, know the manzanita,
the osha,
the path through blue
grama, the black
earth at the water's

edge where she lowers
her jar.
The wind carries word
of upstream. Water drifts down
over the back of her
hand, the fine
hairs on her arm, fingers
sifting river sand.
She gazes beyond
where the brown wren
skitters beneath piñons,
holds what has
always been.

Thieving Flowers

If you had flowers in your
yard I would pick them,
especially the white
daisies and pink
carnations or your
carpet of winedark
mums. It might be
October and yellow
leaves. I'd just walk
by on
any sunny day, my small
scissors tucked back
in a hip pocket, stroll
casually swinging my
arms like I was
out for the fresh
air. If there was no
car at home and the
curtains were closed,
if even the neighbor's
dog did not bark,
I would still be
quick and I would
only cut a
few if you had a
lot and they were
not by the front
door.

The Woman Who Stayed

The time you took my hand
in the dance, touched me
with your eyes, I followed
your lead as you twirled
me out, wrapped me
back and the purple skirt
swirled round my legs.
Your eyes fell on my
husband, and you
whispered: "What has he got
that I don't? Money?"

Or the time you took the corn
from my hands, I was pregnant
working in the field by the
river, irrigating melons,
tomatoes. When you rode up
on your horse, Cactus, his coat
gleamed in the late sun.
"Let me get you some
corn for your dinner."
I left the water
to wander through gold
tassles and rustling green.
I felt the child move as I
picked a few fat ears.
It was in your eyes then
as I handed them up to you.

Again—a later April
the three horse race at Neely's
a track laid out through
rocky pasture. Cactus
balked at the turnaround
sent you flying over yucca
to land on hard ground and
prickly pear. You didn't get up
and I broke from the crowd

ran across the pasture.
They brought your
horse and helped you mount.
When you rode back to our
friends, your eyes sought me.
I knew you'd seen me running.

The time you packed your horses
into the Black Range, winding
up the rocky trail along the
Mimbres, I trailed along
picked wild berries
shared smoked trout on burning
coals beneath the trees
beneath the night. But you were
friend, maybe lover in a different
time, a line that twines where I
cannot see, cannot go
a week with you in the
wilderness (oh the
wildness) of this.

Like Clouds that Come Together and Rain

In a canyon or on a
hillside far from
town we could
sleep in December.

If black branches waved like
dreams above our house, we could
nestle down, almost
drown beneath the rustled

fringe of winter
poplars fanning the river,
the dark knot of cows, their frosty
breath hanging white at dusk.

We could live here, this small
valley, the Indian
ponies that nuzzle the yellow
stubble of grass, try to

nudge it awake. The old wars would
sleep and we would feast like
bears on honeydreams of clear
pools and snapping fish;

even scarred trees
would be cradled in green.

Aging Gracefully

They have weathered rocky
times, these pines, old
crones that sway unsteadily and lurch
in the wind. They lean
on each other for support; with crooked
limb and bony
fingers they point
all ways—
and their low, soughing
moan, like women
who have lost children.
Quiet old gossipers,
more than sap that rises
up the precambium,
and what rushes
watery in the dark cambium
to roots, ringed
memories of men coming and going,
cutting and building and
leaving, the life of
squirrels among branches again,
a constant
watching and bending, shedding of
snow in winter,
they reach for sky,
these grey-
green bearded ladies.

Night at Hidden Lake

Truchas towering to the south,
we climb 14,000 in Sears
tennies, trudge uphill with heavy
packs four miles, past meadows,
finger lakes, columbines and wild
berries. We scrabble
up the steep slope of loose
shale, grabbing at roots and dead
branches of oak. The air cuts sharp.
Pack straps cut.
Our jelly-ankles wobble, angling
down the other side to a smooth
bowl of canyon rock, hasty
lean-to between trees, a quick
fire and collapse. Too tired to play
cards or make love or read
books, beyond speech or
motion we lie while
storm clouds roll in,
the wind whips up, and darkness
draws itself over the lake.

Cupped in the warmth of down
bags we count sleep between
grumblings of some hungry
lord of thunder, drawing his brilliant
sword behind mountains.
One thousand one—
one thousand two—
one thousand three—
flashing it across the churning lake.
One thousand one—
one thousand two—
rumbling boulder walls, growling
omens to bone-weary worn
travellers in the canyon.
One thousand one—

night blazes white. Rain
clicks on our plastic
roof. Our eyelids droop.
If our trees be chosen next,
amen. If this is the end
of life, so be it. Just
give us one last
night of deep, sweet
dreams   drifts
out   on a dark breath of rain.

Boat on a River

Long summer nights we were
the body of an angel, phoenix
rising from twisted
sheets and white ash,
from the first flannel
sheets 16 years ago,
from L.L. Bean with money from tax returns
that should have gone for groceries
or car repairs,
the rosebud delicious
softness bitter nights,
and their oily aroma now
from years of massage.

From the days when you first
built it, something sturdy
for our baby to be born in,
you thought I was getting too
big to heave myself
up from our mattress on the floor,
the trip up the valley to the sawmill,
roughcut pine (all we could afford),
the next two days had you
measuring and sawing, bracing,
and countersinking long bolts.
It was a boat that wouldn't sink
or rock or even
squeak in the roughest of storms.
A bed made for people.
There were six adults on it
at the peak of labor
when I pushed our first son
out into the world.
Among friends.

Our mattress lifted to the level of
windows, vistas from our rock
house on the hillside. I held our child

close in the early November,
the valley blazed,
we drifted in our ship
through yellow and orange, a tangle
of trees,
watched all the leaves fall.

There is no other refuge
or battleground, no other
honeymoon or holy meeting place or even
furniture where we
say with such regularity how this
sure feels good!
sometimes for different
reasons now, with chains of jobs,
kids to peel off the walls,
than in our early seasons
when you were my religion and
your body was my altar.

Now,
when we finally peel our
feet from the floor,
the feel-good sighs are more
for the release of
gravity from our spines
but we worship here still,
and I want you to know
though my words may sometimes say
otherwise,
in my heart—

I don't really want a queensized waterbed,
who needs one when our own
                        bed is a river
                        and a boat on that river,
                        it's the navigator, the stars
by which we travel.

El Hogar

My body could be this narrow
valley curving gold, green-
laced winding to cornfields,
crisp dry pacas,
dusky hermits rustling
parchment skin.

How the water ribbons
down the long canoas
hewn by hand. I could
be these algodones, yellow
giants tossing
coins to ancient priests,
these gentle hills.

The sun slants low across
crumbling adobe,
and it could be me
beating clothes
on rocks in a stream,
squatting
against a bloodwarm wall
to tie my bundles
of gordo lobo
and chamisa.

Our Hands

Just because it was not
me or my hand, but a boy
of six and his mother's frantic
hands, their awful
struggle to wrench him
free when his own hand
stuck in the swimming pool's
drain and drowned him,
her long surfacing, plunging
ache to feed his useless
body, how can it be
business, as usual,
like the ones in Frost's
poem who turned to their affairs
because it was not
their hand, but a luckless
boy who buzzed his
off with the saw and
died when
it should have been supper.

And here,
in this darkened room,
whose hands wringing?
A woman from El Salvador
and her husband being
interviewed from behind bandanas,
saying
they will never go back
where the soil can no longer
absorb the blood,
where they saw their
own baby's throat
slit with a meathook,
even while he was
singing from his
hammock.

In Bread We Trust

We cannot live by bread alone,
especially from the makers of Rainbo
or Mead's fine inflated white
fluff that never knew a
crumb, much less
mold no matter how
stale or old.
Even as civilization rose
out of grains ground on stones
and baked between glowing
coals, so it shall
fall beneath the:
Give us this day our daily
      monocalcium phosphate,
      sodium stearoylactylate,
      ethoxylated mono and
      diglycerides—
      calcium inappropionate.
Even in the back of Lucero's
on Espina Street
where they are making the pan del
muerte for All Souls' Day,
and in the concrete and cinderblock
enterprises
calling themselves bakeries,
it is all dead bread, pale as a
corpse's face, where we should
catch one morning, walking by,
the aroma of wheatfields soaked in
sun and waved around in cool
breezes, the dry chaff of
buckwheat, oats, corn and
rye from the mills and metates of
earth, golden
loaves, body of
Christ, we are taking the name
of Bread in vain.

Accept no substitutes.
Do not be deceived by Mrs. Wright's
caramel-colored light wheat
or even Roman Meal.
Let the memory lingering on our
tongues be rain
and sun on fresh plowed
earth. When there is little
left to believe in, let us
waken the sleeping
yeast, nurture it in embryonic
warmth in the fires
of our own small kitchens. With our own
hands let us raise the house called
Bread, breathe its honest
fragrance and be
filled.